My obsessive compulsive life

Salomón Hayon Zafrany, MD

My obsessive compulsive life

Salomón Hayon Zafrany, MD

EDIQUID

My obsessive compulsive life
© Salomón Hayon Zafrany, MD, 2016
© Ediquid, 2016

October, 2016

Grupo Ígneo
www.ediquid.com
E-mail: contacto@ediquid.com

ISBN: 978-1539575160

Cover Design: Susana Santos

Printed in the United States

Content

Prologue

For several years this book was forged in my mind. Perhaps its beginning was in mid-2007, when I had a clear idea and a name for what was my very particular and strange working manner, which was characterized by a lot of thoughts, worries and immediate actions in pursuit of "perfect order" of material things, checking whether the door was locked or not dozens of times a day, excessive hand washing, among others. It was then that I finally found a name for this: obsessive-compulsive disorder (OCD).

With *My obsessive compulsive life* I have been meaning to try to identify with each of you readers, whether people suffering from this disorder or also those that are identified in one way or another with the work of an obsessive-compulsive. I want to make something clear from the start of these pages: the power or change your lifestyle with less anxiety and be a functional person is in your hands. Apply each of the techniques I present you log in with the best result and see you do that you will achieve a breakthrough in your life.

To my mother, the great lady and feisty, my lifelong hero.

Renee Gilda Zafrany Bentolila deserves every one of the successes that I have been able to achieve in my life. Without it there would be no way, there would be no hope, there would be a person to whom admire. Father and mother to both myself and my brother again.

I am sure that with your help and the positive recognition it may have this book, my mother every reward and personal triumph as his will deserve. Everything I have, everything I am, I owe to her. Thanks Mom.

I love you, and keep fighting.

1. My obsessive compulsive life

My name? Salomón Moisés Gianni Hayon Zafrany. Yes, that's correct, I have three names. Even before my birth the situation was complicated, go figure. And well, what can you expect with the combination of two biblical names and a third of a famous Italian designer. At the end what else is there? One I born and from the first moment one is imposed a name that other person liked. Curiosities of the human race.

But don't you believe that the simple fact of having been named with three names it's a trivial and joyful situation. It has an even deeper meaning, and one that in some cases can be determinant for the cognitive and psychological characteristics of an individual.

I don't like to label myself, or to label others that could be going through or suffering from a psychological disorder, but I do have to admit that I identify myself as "OCD", I mean, in my thoughts and when am asked about the reason of a certain behavior or way of acting, immediately, automatically, internally or externally I phrase: "I'm obsessive compulsive". One way or another, one could see this automatic action as a defense mechanism that the brain generates to protect itself from being pointed as "weird" or different.

It's like that, we are living in a highly competitive world, modern, globalized, in which the stronger, or the ones that adapt better to the changing situations are the ones that will come forward. That's where the people like me that have this disorder start having a complicated life; and when I say life I'm referring to the four spheres that I personally consider essential for every human being: the spiritual sphere, the organic one, the social one and the psychological one. The complication is found in our high degree of mental stiffness, low tolerance to frustration and inflexibility to change. Of course, all this characteristics can be reshaped and soften through time, with strategies that I will present in this book, psychotherapy and, in some necessary cases, medication.

With the spiritual sphere, I refer to all that that motivates you, that moves you, that brings you peace and energy to achieve all that you set your mind to, and that you can be in harmony with your family, yourself, and, why not? With your religion or belief in a divine being. About the organic part, it's all that constitutes the physiology or physical part of the individual, his organs and functioning, lungs, heart, glands, among other things. Following this is the social sphere, referring to all that implies some kind of interaction with other individuals or people with who you can share interests, feelings, emotion, and thoughts; in here we include the family, friends, class or work mates, etc. Last but not least important, given that all the spheres share the same position in a hierarchy, the psychological part is all that I related to your emotion and thoughts, and that can determine your way of acting towards the world that surrounds us.

Four dimensions of human beings

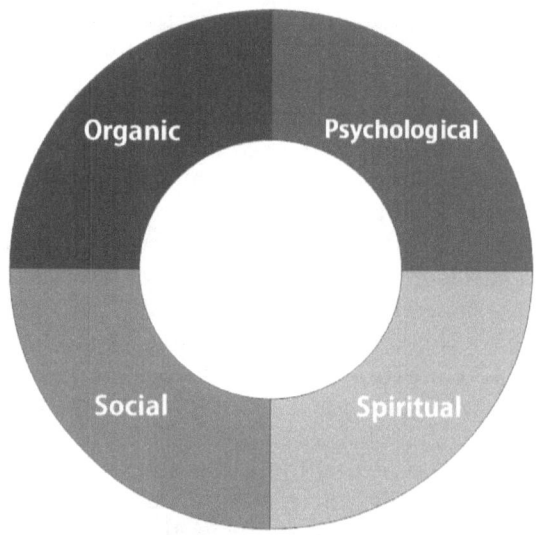

My name is Salomón Moisés Gianni Hayon Zafrany. I live in Costa Rica. In this book, because of its features, a greater attention will be giving to this last part, given that in one way or another, I will how you that we are capable of observing, meditate and identify each of our negative or irrational thoughts, we will also be able to improve the other three spheres and reach our goals in life.

2. Being an OCD

Being an OC, as I say, it's no easy task. I know how much you suffer each day with recurrent thoughts, intrusive and generally irrational that take your anxiety up to the sky.

Now, it's important that we review a little of the theory so we can have the necessary information to identify our obsessions, compulsion and in general all that can imply having OCD, according to the CDC (Center for Disease Control of the USA, 2014) taking in consideration the changes between the Diagnostic and Statistical Manual of Mental Disorders (DSM-IV-TR,2000) in comparision to the DM-5 (2013).

The DSM-5 has some changes in the diagnosis for OCD. In the previous guidelines, the person with OCD had to know that the thoughts or obsessive impulses were only his mind; now, this requirement was eliminated and the diagnosis indicates if the person is convinced that these thoughts and obsessive impulses are real or not.

Now we will present the diagnosis criteria in a brief manner. Please, take into account that they are only here so you can know them and that they must not be used to self diagnose. If you have doubts about any of the symptoms, you must check with certified doctor with experience in the diagnosis and treatment of OCD.

DISCLAIMER: Here are presented said criteria in a simplified manner to make them easy to understand for the general public. It's inclusion in this page have only informational purpose and should not be used to self diagnose. If you have doubts about any of the symptoms, you must check with certified doctor with experience in the diagnosis and treatment of OCD.

To have OCD means to have obsession, compulsions or both.
Obsessions are defined according to the two following aspects:

- Thoughts, impulses and mental images that are constantly repeating themselves. These thoughts, impulses and mental images are unwanted and cause a lot of anxiety or stress.
- The individual that has this thoughts, impulses or mental images tries to ignore them or make them disappear.

- The compulsions are defined according to the two following aspect:
- Repetitive conducts (as an example, washing hands, putting things in an specific order or checking something once and again like when one is constantly verifying if a door is closed) or repetitive thoughts (as an example, praying, counting numbers r repeating word in silence once and again or according to certain rules that must be strictly followed in an rder for the obsession to disappear).
- The purpose of this behaviors or thoughts is to prevent or reduce the angst, or to avoid a feared situation or event. Nonetheless this behaviors or thoughts don't have a relation with the reality of the subject or are clearly exaggerated.

Also, the following conditions must be met:

- The obsessions or compulsions take a lot of time (more than an hour a day), or cause an intense angst or they interfere in a significant manner with the daily activities of the subject.
- The symptoms are not the result of the consumption of a drug or prescribed medicine or any other illness.
- If the subject suffers from another disorder at the same time, the obsessions or compulsions cannot be related only to the symptoms of the additional disorder. By example, to receive the diagnosis of OCD, a person that suffers from a feeding disorder would also have to have obsessions or compulsions that are not related *only* to food.

The diagnosis has to also indicate if the person with OCD understand that the obsessive-compulsive thoughts can be unreal, or if he is convinced that they are real (by example, it's possible that someone knows that it's not necessary to check the kitchen thirty times, but he feels that he has to do it anyway).

The diagnosis has to also indicate if a person with OCD has or has had a twitch. Up to 30% of people with OCD suffer from a twitch their entire lives, especially boys that show symptoms of OCD in their childhood. The people with OCD and twitch disorder have a tendency to differentiate themselves to those without twitch disorder background according to their symptom, the presence of another disorders and the way the OCD manifest itself in the family.

As we can see, the description of OCD can be both simple and complex. If we stick just to the technical part, we will have a very closed and obtuse perspective of this disorder. As a professional I must know this information, but the most important one for me is the one the subject is experiencing and living himself, so I can refer to the theory and be able to reach a clinical diagnose.

I remember when I was little, maybe ten or eleven, when I estimate my obsessive and compulsive traits started manifesting in a more explicit manner. I remember seeing a documentary in the TV in which they showed a kid turning the lights one and off constantly, making checkup ritual and testing the locks of the doors, washing their hands repeatedly, etc. In that moment I told myself: "hmmm, wait, wait, that boy looks like me, would this be the explanation to my thoughts and behaviors?" And, who would have said it? Effectively in the future, even though I suspected it already, that first impression with that documentary was the first realization that I had that the OCD existed.

The OCD has been for me both a blessing and a positive thing. I won't say it has been a curse, I don't want to sound dramatic. The blessing has to do with the aptitudes, skill and mechanisms of cognitive functioning that have pushed me to be a person that's always searching for excellence, abiding by the rule and always finishing my projects. Maybe this profile seems ideal to many in the work sphere, but it isn't, there I a lack of flexibility, creativity, spontaneity and other skills that are sought to fulfill certain work profiles. I have had work opportunities in which my symptoms have been *egosyntonic* (meaning, tuned to my work) and in many others in which they have been egodystonic (meaning, off-key with my personal necessities).

At the student level, in the school, college, I think that the OCD symptoms adhere themselves almost to a perfect degree to the academic environment, it so like that, that I always was a student that was set apart from the rest, and that didn't make me feel good in spite of the perfectionist demand that I stated to my own brain.

In the other side, the not so positive or egodystonic symptoms of OCD have happened or presented to me in social situations, some jobs that search for a less "square" profile, in the family environment, among other situations. All three situations require a certain degree of cognitive flexibility and immediate adaptation, thing that has been up hill for most of my life. Nonetheless, with the passing of years, with the professional, personal and spiritual grow, I have been able to deal in a functional manner with each of these situations.

How have I been able to deal with situations that for us, obsessives and compulsives, are almost impossible? The answer is at the same time easy and complicated. Easy because if we complicate ourselves too much doing so, it's a simple process. Complicated because us, the OCD people, do everything in a complicated manner.

It's as easy as ABC according to the Rational Emotive Behavior Therapy (REBT): everything that happens to us and makes us create a thought about it also creates a conduct or consequence.

By example, A would be the activating event or situation, "I got divorced"; B would be our cognitive process, or the thoughts that such a situation generates in us (A) ("this is the end of the world or the beginning of a better stage in my life"); and C would be the consequences of having thought in an irrational manner as the first thought, or a rational one as the second one; All this according to the activating event or trigger. As such we will have positive and healthy consequences (calm, peace, patience, serenity, joy, etc.) or other negative or ill consequences for our health (anxiety, depression, angst, rage, etc.).

This exercise may seem easy to the bystander, but in practice for us with OCD, when our obsessions are so strong and they are linked to such irrational thoughts, it can be very difficult to apply it, given that one way or another we are creating a certain cognitive flexibility to which we are not accustomed.

This is not the only strategy, there are many more and they also depend on the subject and which suits him better. But let's start with this one and later I will offer you other ones that are highly effective.

The exercise of the ABC of the REBT is at the beginning ideal to be done in a written manner, later and with practice we will do it without needing to put it in paper and almost instantly. This is the beginning of the change, this is the start of the change of or square personality to something more, oval?

3. THE OCD AND THE SENTIMENTAL RELATIONSHIPS

For a person that's highly obsessive and compulsive, with a very organized lifestyle, planned and full of rituals, it's very complicated to establish a lasting sentimental relationship with another person. According to Hayon (2010), the people diagnosed with OCD look one way or another for the other person to eventually adapt to his routines, rituals and/or habits, or at least tries that the other accepts them as a "normal" situation. We all know that for a sentimental relationship to be successful both parts must accept each other, and there must be a certain degree of flexibility in each individual for this to happen. In the case of a person with OCD, this one tries for the other person to be the lead character in the change and for him to adapt to every, or most of the behaviors that the subject with OCD presents. This doesn't augur a positive result, given that in my experience these adaptations that the other person does last for a short period of time, and that eventually this person tires and asks a person with OCD to change (something that him or her eventually refuses to do and the relationship in most cases ends).

But then the question of "I as an OC, Can I have a lasting and happy sentimental relationship?" the answer is, it depends. It depends on if you are willing or not to sacrifice part of your OCD behaviors and make flexible certain thought patterns and try to think in a more rational manner that benefits the relationship. Are you willing to do so? Then you can have a meaningful and lasting sentimental relationship with someone. It's not easy but it is possible. Your companion must also understand all your particularities and one way or another accept you with all your "defects" and positive aspects. If both parts are honest, sincere and there is true love, then all these obstacles can be solved. This is not a secret, everyone knows, but we don't apply this in a rational and healthy manner.

In my personal experience, the sentimental relationships that I have had tend to have a determined time of existence, determined by the patience and the limits that the other person to rest certain behavior and thought patterns that are both new and different to those she has encountered. My main difficulties when I have been in a relationship have been the rigidity when it comes to eating with someone else (I like to eat alone and what I usually eat), dates and time to see each other (I'm not a morning person and day are determined by the fulfillment or not of my gym routine, for example), sleeping together the whole night (ideally I prefer to sleep by myself after sex), sharing the morning routine of going to the bathroom, taking a shower, dressing up (that is something in which I need my privacy and don't like to share, it would give me too much anxiety). As we see, there are many and I could give even more details, and what we can see from each of these behaviors and thoughts in general are that these are rigid routine patterns, repetitive and irrational that bring as a consequence great amounts of anxiety and avoid conducts (remember the ABC?).

4. THE POSTIVE SIDE OF HAVING OCD

It's true that we obsessives and compulsives have many "negative" aspects that generate us a great quantity of anxiety and uncomfortable feelings, but there is also a wide spectrum of positive aspects and strengths that we can recover from our cognitive and conduct characteristics, that can favor us from day to day.

Next I present several examples and situations in which we can apply our charcteristics:

- **Organization:** we are capable of organizing almost everything that is around us, from our houses, work, studies, chores, moving, etc. We know everything that is needed or required to achieve with success each of these activities. We are methodical and systematic in organizing our activities in priority order.
- **Control:** we can be capable of controlling almost completely our interior and our environment. It's true that sometimes we are filled with intrusive thoughts, but also it's true that by learning certain techniques we can be capable of giving priority to those functional and positive thoughts and leave behind the dysfunctional and negative ones. To achieve this is necessary to do the ABC continuously and right.
- **Persuasion:** given our high analysis capability of the personal and external circumstances that surround other individuals, we can persuade many people and situations to our favor. This must be used for our sake and without harming others, because our selfishness and self-absorption sometimes we can hurt others as long as we benefit ourselves.
- **Excellence:** we have the capacity to exceed the expectations of a situation, project or any field in which we develop. It's not difficult to feel satisfied with mediocrity. According to Hayon (2010) the people with OCD have an IQ from 5 to 10 points above average.

We the OC are complex by nature, but incredible enough even so we still have the will and irrationality to complicate our lives further. Something as simple as having an appointment the next day, or a meeting, from the moment that we are given the information we start to plan, thinking in the future, projecting different stages, etc, I mean, we fill everything with mental labels that produce a great anxiety for an specific fact or event that by itself its part of the routine of most human beings.

The positive side of being OCD			
Organization	Control	Persuasion	Excellence

It's like a paradox, we want that life and thoughts to be simplified to have less degrees of anxiety, but at the same time automatically, I repeat, **irrationally**, we predispose ourselves with too many mental loads to an specific situation, which sometimes produces us so much anxiety that we avoid it, we don't do it and afterwards we feel guilty because of that. Who can understand us? Well, I do and for that am here, to try to help, as I have helped myself.

This is a petition that I make to you my fellow OC, please let's try to stay in the present moment, in the now, in the **right now!**, at least a 60 to 70 % of the time in which we are conscious and thinking during the day. The rest of the day, the 30 to 40 % its permitted to have your future and/or past thoughts.

5. Administration of irrational thoughts

It's in this part in which I want to introduce you another useful tool that will serve to manage the amount of time that we spent traveling in thought between the past and the future. This tool I call "the OCD clock", that basically is to use our great planning and self-imposing skills, to program certain hours of the day, 15 minutes every 4 hours, in which we can be as OC as we can, thinking in the future, past being **irrationaln,** etc. But after these 15 minutes we stop, we set a pause and we wait 4 hours till our next opportunity to be free.

The purpose of this tool is that we try to live in the present moment most of the day and to have a max total of 2 hours daily to have obsessive or irrational thought.

Here an example:

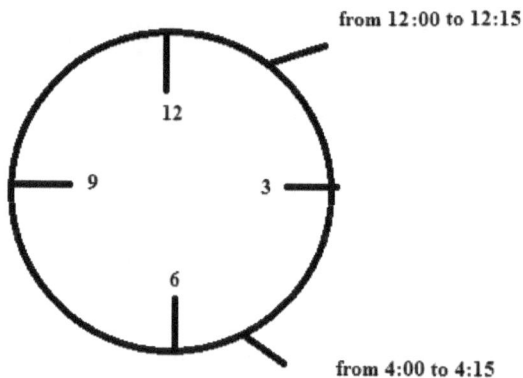

from 12:00 to 12:15

from 4:00 to 4:15

Here we see a normal clock of 24 hours. We decide to tart this exercise at 12 pm, then from 12 pm to 12:15 pm, I can be as obsessive and compulsive as I want, as irrational as I desire, thinking in the future and past, fill myself with anxiety, etc. You can use the 15 minutes completely or stop when you see fit, but when you decide to stop or the 15 minutes are up you cannot continue with those thoughts, and you have to remain in the present, **in the now**, for 4 hours (technically 3 hrs and 45 min) till you the net 15 minute window is up and you can be obsessive, like this, at 4 pm you can go back to being obsessive and irrational for 15 minutes. And like this the cycle repeats itself every 4 hours each day, even in the night and you have the window open and you can wake up to be obsessive.

What's the result of this?

According to my experience with many patients to which I have introduced to this technique, you get a dramatic reduction in the quantity, frequency and intensity of the obsessions, irrationalities and mental escapes towards the future and past, which equals to peace, tranquility and living in the present (no PRE/occupations = occupied before time).

Remember this and all the other strategies that I have presented you and I will keep on presenting you, are essential to be able to deal with the overload of thoughts that you have in those moments. I don't ask you to use all of them, but to choose two or three that you know really well how to use and that work for you. I understand that you can be skeptical of some techniques, I was as well, but until you use them and practice them and see the positive results for your health, you cannot make a real appreciation about them and their efficiency. **Be patient (peace + science = science of peace).**

It's incredible how we the OC are in many times in a useless quest for calming our thoughts, but at the same time, when we find a way out, a tool or a technique, we put a mental label on it, we use irrational explanations and in general we act like I have said many times before, passing from a relatively easy process to something incredibly complicated.

6. THE PROFESSIONAL HELP

This is a very important point for my life and it has been the starting point of this incredible, complicated, sad, happy, anxious joyful, depressive and hopeful journey, since I decided to search professional help with my psychologist and psychiatrist.

Between the end of 2006 and the beginning of 2007 I started my search for professional help, to soothe this huge current of anxious thoughts that didn't let me live in peace. First I got an appointment with my psychologist the master Ana Catalina Vargas, specialist in REBT and my first great help in this improvement journey. Being honest I didn't actually believe it was going to help me, but it did and I took back my thoughts. As a true professional she did a first interview to learn essential basic data, then she did a series of psychological tests that resulted in my first and official diagnosis that yes, me, Salomón Moisés Gianni Hayon Zafrany, had OCD!

This diagnosis I took with calm and anxiety at the same time. Calm because it gave an explanation to all that I felt, and anxiety because I knew I had to do something, if not my life was going to continue in a pattern of irrationalities and anxieties that were killing me.

Knowing that the treatment of this disorder, as in most health issues and other psychological disorders, needs an interdisciplinary approach, I went to the Dr. Itzel Pérez Pérez, my psyquitrist. My first session as also an initial interview and she already had contact with Catalina and knew of the result of my tests, even though she made extra tests to confirm the diagnosis.

RESULT?

I HAVE OCD!

Then it came the part in which she was specialized, the medication, in this case:

- Fluvoxamine maleate (Luvox antidepressant, inhibiter of the serotonin absortion).
- Alprazolam (benzodiazepine anxiolytic). In the case of the Luvox we started with 100mg and with 1mg of Tafil.

That was my medication for about four years, afterwards we change the Luvox for Fluoxetine and I have maintained myself like that as well as with the Tafil for years till today.

Is medication important? Is important that goes along of a psychological process? The answers are **yes** and **yes**. There isn't another road as efficient, don't do as we do to try to explain and pull an ace up our sleeve and try to look for the cats fifth leg. Ladies and gentleman, lets accept this as the first and right step. I emphasize: **let's accept** and **resign ourselves** to this process. These are two powerful words that will set you free of the useless fight and bring you peace.

You want my honest advice? Look for a good psychologist and psychiatrist, experts in the subject. Do your homework, investigate, we are excellent at it and once you have chosen your professionals, accept their recommendation and prescriptions without thinking too much about it… **Do not obsess compulsively over something that will soothe your OCD!** In general the base treatment it's a combination between an antidepressant (called like that because of their category but in general is an obsessiveness reducer) and an anxiolytic to help reduce the anxiousness. In today's market there is a great variety and it will depend in the professional's criteria which of them make the best med combination for you.

7. Flexibility in solid mental structures in OCD

My intention has always been to make it in a spontaneous manner without **obligations.** It seems like a paradox. I have wanted to write my book about obsessiveness in the least obsessive manner. And this is something that I want to revisit so we can emphasize it in this process of knowing how to live in a "harmonious" manner with our OCD. But it's the reality and an exercise of mental flexibility that we must do little by little. You already have very defined structures, obsessions and compulsions, how about we try to have another activities and responsibilities that **we want to do when we want to do them**? And not in a obligated rigid manner as most things we do daily, I promise you will enjoy it!

The obsessiveness, the structure, the planning, all that helps us to drain thoughts, but it doesn't bring us peace and tranquility, and if it does it's just a matter of minutes till you are repeating yourself, repeating over and over your functioning schemes. I don't ask you to stop planning and having functioning parameters well defined, it would be false given that I also do it, what I need from you is that you add to that rigidness, anxiety and worry, a little of disorder, spontaneity, diversion and no planning, what do you think? **Do it**, don't think about it!

Talking about the defects and virtues that we have as OC, I want to start using certain patterns and characteristics of our personality that we think as negative, in something positive and productive. That's what I call an assertive channeling of our obsessions.

8. FORGIVING AND ADMITING MISTAKES

You know me already, I ump form a subject to another, according to my emotional and situational state. This part for me is especially important, the part in which we admit we are wrong, or in my case, we exceed ourselves emotionally, and being capable of admitting the irrationality of our conduct and apologize. If the other person accepts the apology and forgives us, better yet, but the important part is that you do what's right. You cannot control what the other person will perceive or say.

This subject comes up because I have **identified** in myself (one of the principal tools to modify **irrationalities**, the identification) that when I believe I'm right, I defend it from the beginning with claw and teeth, no matter the feelings and circumstances of others. This is something in which I have been working and trying to correct to avoid it happening again. My main trigger for this type of conducts and reactions overreacted, is when the manager of some clinic or institution doesn't pay me in time, after I have accomplished in a **precise, organized and excellent** manner (as a proper OC) my professional commitment with patients. Do you understand me? Our armor of precision, exactitude and punctuality, it's completely affected when it clashes with its opposite pole, the disorganization, unpunctuality, deceives, etc. It's like they produced a short circuit between our values and the OCD behavior against other person that doesn't honor his responsibilities.

I emphasize this because it has happened to us before, it happens right now and it will continue to happen, we will encounter many personalities like this one, but we must be conscious that not everyone shares the same kind of OCD as we do, and because of that we must have patience, use the ABC, positively channel our obsessions and use one of our best tools as I said before: **persuasion**. If we use this resource with which we are excellent with the objective of having the results that we want, instead of exploding and doing conducts that bring us more negative consequences we could have positive ones.

9. THE ISOLATION AS A DEFENSE MECHANISM

There are many defense mechanisms that we usually hear daily, for example, denial, rationalization, projection, etc. All this comes from the times of Sigmund Freud, one of the fathers and pioneers of psychology and psychoanalysis. But in this subject that has to do with us, I don't want to make it complicated, let's talk about the **isolation** (yes, effectively, while I write this fragment I'm isolated and in hermit mode) Why do I bring this up? I bring it up because our mind already works to the maximum 24 hours a day, with overwhelming thoughts, intrusive ones, anxious ones, visualizing the future, the past, all that we have already been talking. The isolation is a tendency or behavior that we use as a way to "stop" ourselves from this overload of thoughts. We go and lock ourselves in our house our room and we try to arrange our ideas, and if we already have learned how to use certain techniques, this space serves to discard the irrational and think about the rational. With this kind of behavior what we intensively search is to stop the load of external stimuli (people, environment, etc.) as much as we can, especially what we see or hear. For us this is a temporary solution that we want to work and for its effect to last longer as much as we can, but reality is that this is just a limited scape from our thoughts.

This places tends to be ones room, the living room, a park without people or even a bathroom (at least it works for me). We hide ourselves in our shell and we start to analyze our thoughts like we were a computer antivirus, and as in everything in life, if the antivirus is updated, it's trustworthy and work correctly, it will register the possible threats and eliminate them. The same thing happens to our mind and this comparison that we just did. What happens is that most times our brain antivirus, to be able to detect the irrational thoughts, tends to be hacked and outdated, of unknown origin and working badly.

My recommendation in these cases if we are accustomed to doing this kind of behavior and at the same time we have to deal with family, professional and social life, is that we include in our routine the tool of the **OCD watch,** explained before. We choose a peaceful place in which we feel good and we can analyze, even if its irrational, for 15 minutes, and later we come out like nothing happened. This strategy will diminish the frequency, intensity and uncomfortable feeling of irrational thoughts.

Another option is to do what I call the **paradox of exposure to anxiety.** Is as simple as when we feel like running and going to our safe place, we do exactly opposite, we expose ourselves more, we interact with more people, we go to places filled with people, etc. How does this help? Given that when we refuse the brain from its intention to hide, it doesn't have another option that to pay attention to a new quantity of stimuli that it didn't foresee, and because of that it will have to leave behind some of the **irrational** thoughts for which it wanted to isolate itself. This tool only works if practiced many times and you don't give up. Remember that the brain is a like a muscle that has to be trained constantly and has to be surprised with new experiences for it to grow stronger.

10. OCD AND MEDICATION

Disclaimer: what I will expose now is my personal and professional experience, knowledge about biochemistry in meds and their combinations that can serves alongside therapy, as long as we go to our psychiatrist or trusted physician that authorizes us.

In nowadays pharmaceutical market there is a huge variety of sizes, colors, prices, tastes and all kind of meds that can help us **or harm us** if we don't follow the doctor's orders.

In general the meds and their combinations that I will expose with their generic name, in a manner of options and in line of their order of choice, are or can be antidepressants, anxiolytics, mood regulators, among others. I will not indicate dosage given that is very subjective according to the person and their tolerance.

1. Fluvoxamine maleate + alprazolam (or diazepam, or clonazepam)
2. Fluoxetine + alprazolam (or diazepam, or clonazepam)
3. Clomipramine (o imipramine) + alprazolam (or diazepam, or clonazepam)
4. Valproic acid + alprazolam (or diazepam or clonazepam)

What I just exposed would be my options list that I could use to, eventually, in case of being necessary, administrate medication to a patient. Nonetheless this list can be changed depending in the many subjective variables of an individual. There also exist other medical criteria that must be respected, as long as they are well based.

11. TECHNIQUE OF "GO WITH THE FLOW"

There are days or moments of these days in which we are or become more obsessive than usual. They can happen without notice and a hundred thoughts can happen **without** end, most of them rational but another percentage **irrational**. I emphasize these last ones because I have said before, those are the ones that we need to hear and pay notice most of the times. In these times in which our OCD is mode **on** and drunk with Red Bull, I suggest to rescue the technique of thought filter, detecting the rational ones and then extrapolating their utility and magnitude. What we will accomplish in this case, what I suggest, it's that we do that filter process in a detailed manner and that we list all those rational thoughts and act **obsessively** about them. In this manner we will leave behind the irrationality and we will act on an obsessive and compulsive manner but rationally.

12. DELAY THE REWARD OR INMEDIATE GRATIFICATION

This is a subject of cognitive and behavior psychology that has many implications in a variety of situations, disorders and behaviors. So I am *properly* understood: the delay of the instant gratification or reward by any action or thought is key for **your health and that of your loved ones**, and that of the rest of the world. Having **patience (peace-science)** it's fundamental to reach all the objectives that you have planned for your life, to be peaceful, to reach peace of mind states unimaginable, to live **happily,** etc. **Calm!** All in due time, even more so for us with OCD, us that want everything to happen immediately as long as we get our mental peace that in reality it's only momentary and fictional. If you really want that thought and action to disappear, you have to stop it, delay it and change it for a more productive and rational thought that is not a reflection of a useless and senseless cognitive reaction.

But how? Just doing it, stop delaying the use of the techniques I'm teaching you, getting out of your comfort zone and dealing with your fear and ghosts, facing the anxiety and telling it: "I'm right where and I recognize you, I know how you are and I know how to control you". You are armed my friend, you have all the tools to defeat this anxiety that you yourself have created. **You created it yourself, you are going to eliminate it,** alright? Try to understand what you are reading. That thing that you are so afraid of, that thing that you believe is so unknown, it's simply a completely irrational creation made by your super-active mind. Us that have OCD are extremely intelligent to recognize, identify and transform an irrational thought and behavior in the most healthy and rational thing. AND YES! I WILL REPEAT IT TILL YOU GET TIRED AND UNDERSTAND IT!

13. THE ABILITIES OF THE OCD TO MANIPULATE AND/ OR CONVINCE OF IT'S USE

We agree that the obsessive and compulsive individual eventually has to face situations and scenarios in its life that do not work with a structured and rigid life plan. If you are like me then you have experienced that all the situations and events in which we develop ourselves we want to mold them to our convenience, and we spend hours and days working in a strategy to get away with it. This can happen in our work, studies, reunions, appointments, etc. We try to stop all those situations to break from our established pattern of routines, that can have particular schedules, activities or situations that are not compatible with our life scheme.

In my particular case this happens to me constantly at work with my schedule and particular activities that I have to do that affect my obsessions and compulsions. For example, I'm not a morning person, so if I have an appointment, meeting or dates in the morning, I look for any excuse possible to move them to the afternoon. I spent hours and days previous to the date looking for excuses to move the schedule. Another thing would be for example that, sometimes there are some activities related to food, social events, etc.

Activities to which I'm completely allergic and take my anxiety to a thousand degrees, because I have very rigid eating patterns, and in those kind of situations sometimes you have to play some sport or do a physical activity that I don't like to do, because I would start sweating, I would be uncomfortable and I would prefer to fly away like a combat plane in an emergency. I do and can do physical activities when I plane it, dress for it and its part of my usual routine.

From this I try to escape, and I spend hours and hours working out the escape plan and the excuses to get away with it. It's something tiresome and that has produced me a lot of anxiety during my life, given that it takes away spontaneity, flexibility and happiness.

14. TO PERSEVERE
OR TO GIVE UP?

One of the most difficult things to us is to persevere and not give up to the activities or situations that have to do with anxiety, uncertainty and that in general are out of our well planned plans. I have to confess that I have given up many times, sometimes without major consequences and others with a great weight in my conscience. At the end when I reflect upon it, I generally regret having giving up and renounced to stay in my comfort zone. I know, is a crossroad and a very difficult decision to make. To continue with what we know is "right" or to give up so we don't have to face our fears and ghosts. I recommend something, before giving up think about it twice and visualize yourself in the future thinking about if you will regret or not such decision, given that generally there is no turning back. This will sound like a cliché, but to give up something, a situation or a person because we know is "right" will hurt us the rest of our lives, but to stay there, to continue no matter how uncomfortable it is sometimes, will give us a reward later that will overcome any inconvenient or uncomfortableness that we have had.

Let's not lie to ourselves and say that the renounce doesn't feel as good, given that everyone that is reading this book have felt that release and momentary peace. It's a freedom that is momentary, because I'm sure that you have asked yourself many times "What would have happened if…?" Well, the only answer for that question can be found by staying, insisting and continuing in that which you consider good and correct for your life.

I want to add that this last text I did it in a moment in which I really wanted to give up to my job. Part of this job at the moment that I'm writing this lines, doesn't only have to do with helping professionally a group of teenager students in the United States, but also once a month, more and less, to take them in an "adventure" to some place in Costa Rica. Of course this "adventure" it's more of a "tragedy" filled with anxiety, worries and places completely out of my comfort zone, which represent a great dilemma for me, because it makes me question if I continue or not in my work, and if I think rationally, realistically and "right" is a place in which I must be, given that the pay is well, it has to do with my profession and makes me face challenges that ideally would improve my quality of life as someone with OCD and as a human. For the moment I listened to myself and the words I wrote in the past paragraph, and after a few days it has sense to continue here and fight against my "demons", which I personally created.

One of the strategies that helped me the most was to put myself in **acceptance** mode, and more than this I would say **resignation**, because it's that moment in which you have to stop fighting against that which is happening in reality and accept it with open arms. This technique would permit you to stop rolling around hypothetical or possible scape scenarios and exits that turn into a unending obsession filled with anxiety, and if I had listen to it, I would possibly have suffered some consequences in my job or I would have resigned; and as I said before, this job for me is the right thing to do in this moment of my life, to resign would be to completely agree with my OCD and the irrationality to then suffer the consequences of guilt and frustration.

The temptation of giving up and go to our comfort zone immediately is very attractive and actually produces a certain calm just by thinking in being able to be in that state. What happens is that said scenario that we picture with calm and peace is false, and we know it perfectly well; it's simply a state in which we won't have the responsibility that we want to run from, but this will be accompanied for another series of obsessions and situations that will contribute to a big load of anxiety and the sense of guilt of having resigned to the "right" thing to do. I have said many times now this "right" word because is the one that best describes what I'm trying to express. It's a situation in which we have to be and must accomplish if we want to move forward in life.

15. THE TECHNIQUE OF THE HORSE AND THE RIDER

There is a technique that I have been using lately that I have named **the horse and the rider.** This phrase I pull from my memory from when I was studding psychology and I was explained in my psychoanalysis classes that the I, was the conscious part of our mental sphere, and that it was like a rider that took the reins of a horse and gave it direction and orders. More or less that's where I'm coming from but with some modifications. I imagine that I am the combination of a horse with its rider that are intimately connected and integrated. This horse has the capacity of free action and it's the job of the rider to give him orders and guide him for him to work or develop in the most "healthy" and efficient manner. This works especially when I have to do various activities or jobs during the day. The horse and the rider already know all they have to do, but the horse is basically or simply the engine or active being that mobilizes towards the actions, the rider I the one that performs the delicate plays and takes the reins about when to do each thing and how to do them, he also has the power to calm the horse when this is agitated or anxious with a small pet in the head. Let's say that he has the capacity to be the guide and manipulator of each and all the actions and sensations of the horse, and as such he can determine that the horse accomplishes all the activities that he has assigned in the most effective and calm manner for him. For example, when I'm taking a shower and washing my face the anxiety generally climbs, in that moment I picture the horse agitated and he needs the calm of the rider and for him to tight the reins a little so he can keep the activity that he was performing. It's a mixture of giving a small caress to the horse but at the same time tighten the course so the intention is no diverted in futile and unnecessary things with little productivity.

As such, during the day I picture that I'm that horse and at the same time that rider going alongside accomplishing activities and every time they want to divert the course y apply a caress and a little tightening of the reins.

16. THE UNCONFORTABLENESS CAUSE BY ONESELF

There are so many things that we want to control and to work under our strict cognitive system, that sometimes this overly rigid normality produces an opposite effect that produces a discomfort and general anxiety. For example, have the tendency that if I'm going to some place in which my general scheme of functioning is not compatible, I may take some meds to lower my level of anxiety; nonetheless the simple fact of taking a med produces anxiety, considering the possible side effects like stomach issues (which are n my top 3 of anxieties). See why I mean? Sometimes our "cure" has even more problems than the original situation, reason which the moral of this fable is like the saying: if it's not broken, DON'T FIX IT.

One of the things I have always asked myself is how my life would be without OCD. Would it be easier, harder, what would I do or a living, etc? Of course like this we would start with the trips to the past that I have emphasized are not positive, those in which we ask what if... If I really try to imagine my life with different behavior and thought patterns, a more relaxed personality, a more "normal" life style, actually it's hard for me to eventually see myself in these situations. I don't know why but the Salomón that lives and breathes today is the Salomón that I have always wanted to be, and yes, I have suffered a lot of anxieties and stressfull situations in mi life, but I believe that if I put it all in a scale, this one will turn to all the things that this life has given me. With this I want to make you understand that our positive process of resignation about how we are, in which we accept why we are here and the wonderful human beings that we are just like we are and how our parents brought us into this world, it's a vital key in the process of living better each day.

17. SEEKING HELP

To have OCD and not ask for help is the perfect combination to our psychological downfall and defeat as human beings in general. The first cry for help that we have to ask is to ourselves, is to ask permission to ask for help and telling someone what is happening to us, and then let this people do their work and help us. Many times we don't dare to ask for help because we consider that our problems are too weird for other people to understand them, besides we don't want to seem like weird people. The issue is that I assure you that you can find more open arms available to help you than you imagine. It's here when we have to stop being selfish, self-centered and lower our defenses and let our loved ones or trusted people to which we are telling what is happening to us, to just do their job and eventually benefit us.

The kind of help that we have to focus on asking has to be constructed by two main characteristics. First, one or more trusted individuals, people with who we don't have problems telling all that we want, and the other kind of help is the professional one, that has to be made out by a psychologist and a psychiatrist. In the first case, this person or group of people has to provide you with the necessary security for you to be able to tell them what is happening, they have to be able to react in a rational and productive manner for you. They must be people that you know really well and that you now their response mechanism to various situations, they can be your parents, friends, relatives, etc. In the case of the professional help, this one must come from experts in the subject. Do not go with the first psychologist or psychiatrist that you find, I want you to be obsessive looking for the best professional and the best with who you can eventually open yourself in a therapy and psychological process of recovery and improvement of your life.

18. ANXIETY AS AN ALLY?

Yes, you are not misreading, if we want to go forward in this process that will last all our life, we have to accept that high but working levels of anxiety will be with us for the rest of it. Stop! Do not throw this book to the garbage and ask yourself why are you reading this book and going to therapy, etc. You are doing that because such is life and it has as many beautiful and positive things as others that are not, but I assure you that at the end: to do the journey through this experiences that are not so positive, will leave you with a huge satisfaction and pride that cannot be compared not even with a life filled with happiness. What I always say is: "to be happy you have to always be tricking anxiety and depression" and as such accepting our best friend/enemy: **anxiety!**

There is something really interesting in us with OCD, and is that in some manner we seem masochists. Yes, it seems like we cannot live without the pain of anxiety, even if we say that we want no more, what we do is acquire it for free every day and every moment. Then I ask you, do you really hate anxiety that much? And if it's like that, why do you create irrational thoughts by yourself, that come up with a load of angst and nervousness? That's why I don't want you to keep picturing yourself as the victim of anxiety. Even if it's true that we have certain natural disposition to be more anxious than others, a great percentage of that anxiety that makes you uncomfortable you created it yourself, you saw it being born, grow and you let it take over you. And like you permitted all of that to happen, you are also capable of defeating it and see it disappear if you set your mind to it, using the different techniques that I show you in this book. It's enough of having secondary profit, and the "poor guy he suffers anxiety", it's enough! Tight those pants right and use that capacity of battling working cognitions and try to eliminate each of those thoughts that have no room in your life and are working against your happiness.

19. TRANSFORM YOUR CAPACITY TO ANTICIPATE AND PLAN IN AN ALLY

We are the best people to foresee situations, sometimes we nail it sometimes we don't, but the important thing is that we are good for this activity. Even if it's true that a lot of what we see coming has little use and generates anxiety, and because of that what we are going to do from now onwards is channeling if a productive manner the foreseeing processes and the capacity to visualize the future in our advantage. I give you an example, if you have business trip and you need to take some things like clothes, documents for a meeting, your computer, bathing stuff, make the reservations for different places, etc. All of that makes common people forget something and that can be bad for their trip. In our case we make sure of doing a *checklist* of all the things that we need, but I need you to write it with the objective of letting go of all those thoughts in a piece of paper, so they are not roaming and messing around in your head. If you have this trip in two weeks' time, don't leave the preparation for the last minute, do the *checklist* first and accomplish each of the necessary activities for the trip little by little, till you accomplish everything with enough time before the journey to be able to be relaxed about it. That's why I ask you that from today onwards when you foresee and plan something for the future, I want you to do this:

1. Be certain that the situation requires planning.
2. Do a *checklist* of things to be done.
3. Start doing the chores step by step with enough time.

20. THE TEMPTATION OF USING MORE POTENT DRUGS

Once medicated and with our capacity of searching for information and being obsessive in the search for meds that have a greater effect, we can find ourselves with the diatribe and temptation of using drugs that are not specified for the OCD, but that have a great potential to relax and calm, two of the main ingredients that we with OCD search for every day. When one finds a new drug or med that gives us mental peace and calm there is high chance that we become addicted to it, given that we are so overwhelmed with thoughts, that finding a solution even if temporary is highly enticing for us. I bring this up because I have had patients with OCD that have become addicted to morphine and other opioid drugs for their great relaxation and anxiety inhibition capacity.

One of the challenges of having OCD is to have the urge to listen to what is "right", it's how difficult is for us to make certain routines or behaviors more malleable and at the same time to make the change that let us keep our work, arrive at an appointment or eat at a determined time of day, etc. (I mean, to do new "right" activities that change your routine). Right now while I write these lines in my work place I have to go out on a trip or an adventure, to a location in the beach in which we will perform certain community labor, and in where it will be impossible for me to accomplish all my routines. This is an activity that I have to do to keep my job that is "right" for me. One of the things that is more difficult for me is trying to make my food patterns malleable and also to generally develop **higher tolerance frustration patterns,** something I have faced before.

The tolerance to frustration is the key to determine how capable we are to keep our day to day, our routine, without using help, a shortcut and in general, beng capable of delaying the gratification.

THOUGHT RECORD

This exercise will permit us to record our main thoughts or those that produce anxiety during our day and then analyze them with the ABC, identifying the rational from the irrational like we explained before:

Thought 1:

A:_____
B: _____
C: _____

Thought 2:

A: _____
B: _____
C: _____

Thought 3:

A: _____
B: _____
C: _____

Thought 4:

A: _____
B: _____
C: _____

Thought 5:

A: _____
B: _____
C: _____

Today onwards you can do it in black pages at any time of the day and also when you need to apply a rational tone to your cognitive system.

This exercise will be more effective the more you do it, and eventually you will be able to do it in your head and almost automatically. I want you to realize when you are writing the irrational part down and the lack of evidence in your thoughts till the point in which you can laugh of all the "silliness" that you were thinking and that were producing negative consequences.

One way or another I want you to understand that most of your negative feelings and emotions are produced by this kind of thought that has no anchor in reality and that are completely futile.

21. THE RELIGIOUS AND/OR SPIRITUAL TECHNIQUE

For those of us that express our religion, in my case Judaism, there are different prayers that are very powerful and meaningful for a person, like for example, the *Holy Father* for Christians, the *Shema Israelk* for jews, and other ones that are very important in the different religions that people practice. It doesn't have to be a religious phrase or set of words the ones we are going to repeat constantly. They can be motivational affirmations, little speeches that fulfill you and reach you, among other things.

What I want from this technique is that when we are full with intrusive thoughts, uncomfortable and irrational ones that produces a lot of anxiety, we repeat this prayer or motivational phrase, as many times as it's necessary so you can finish the activity that you were doing. You will see that this phrase is going to set you free from many of those thoughts that are making you uncomfortable and not letting you do your work with calm, peace and effectively. Little by little you will realize that this exercise will be very useful when intrusive thought attack you without notice. Try and see.

22. I COULDN'T DO IT ANYMORE

At last I couldn't do it anymore, I couldn't continue with the job that I was telling you was the "right one" for me and that I was fighting against my discomfort and obsessive thoughts. Believe me, I tried my hardest and tried to use all the techniques so far, but I couldn't, I gave up. At the end I don't feel as guilty because my physical integrity was at risk, because I didn't feel able to handle certain environmental conditions that were present in the aforementioned "adventure" or tragedy for me. A heat that was close to the 40 degrees, not properly hydrated or fed, scarce sanitary conditions, few hours to sleep, not being able to do my physiological needs, etc. There were too many things in my plate that I couldn't handle and I had to give up. What do I do now? Well I continue to fight as I have always done so and even if my obsessive thoughts have grown with the "what if..." or the "what would have happened..." I know it was the right decision for that moment of my life and my health, and now I support my spiritual side knowing that my god will have something better for me.

I have to admit that the little percentage of guilt and pressure that I'm imposing in myself has affected me and escalated my general levels of anxiety and obsession. A very old pot loaded with thoughts related with work is opened. The whole process of being hired in this country (Costa Rica) for the profession I studied is hard, even harder in the case of the psychologists, we are the third or fourth profession with more professional unemployed people. Retaking writing has helped me because it works as a catalyzer and catharsis for these obsessions that are unproductive and unhealthy for my integrity. These are the moments in which I have to retake my trust and my capacity to say "yes, I have been there and I came unscathed", it's here where being extra careful with my irrational thoughts and bend towards the voices of rationality most of the time works, sanity and patience, voices that will open again the door to a work field that's adequate to my skills.

23. HAVING OCD AND WORK RELATIONS

Having OCD and exercising a profession or job is complicated, because we know that all the work conditions for which we have been hired could welcome certain obsessions, compulsions, rituals, etc. It's here where a lot of factors have to be considered, which can be: necessity to work or economic necessity, attitude and enthusiasm towards the position, and maybe what's more important, the disposition to be flexible and to change for professional success. This last element is crucial and very hard to establish in reality, because one can have the great disposition to change, to be flexible, to leave certain behavioral and cognitive patterns behind, and another element is the reality of having OCD and being capable of actually doing it. "from the theory to the practice, having OCD, there's a great distance".

24. GUILT, ANXIETY AND REMORSE FEELINGS

Every proper person with OCD feels these emotions. The guilt is a major component in our days, be it because we couldn't do our established routine, or on the contrary, feeling guilty because we left our people and loved ones in a secondary position compared to our obsession. About remorse, this one has the characteristic of mental journeys to the past using the "if I had…" phrase. My friend, the past is there in a timeline that cannot be tweaked no more, just like the future is untouchable. Here I repeat the importance of keeping ourselves in the now, in the present. Let me tell you something, that remorse that you have now, besides causing you anxiety and not being good for you, it's completely irrational and has no bases. The facts or actions for which you are feeling guilt and remorse were situations in which you reacted according to your skills and resources at the time. Maybe now with more experience, *insight* and information, you could act differently, but that is the past, take advantage now of this new level of knowledge that you have to provide yourself with more accurate and beneficial answers.

I will like you to make a list now of five situations in which you feel guilt or remorse and analyze it with the ABC technique, identifying irrational thought patterns and also doing yourself a test of the conditions that you had in that moment for you to act in that manner. At the end of the exercise I want you to pay special attention to the irrational thought patterns and their connection with the negative consequences. You will realize that in the present, acquiring new knowledge and techniques such as these, the response method would have been completely different, full of rationality and positive conviction in our thoughts and actions.

25. OUR SACRED PLACE

During my practice as a professional and in my own experience in OCD, I have found a common factor that has always spiked my attention, and it has to do with a sacred place, indestructible and with a great sentimental value for us, in which we will feel free and without worries of being watched, judged or labeled. This place in my personal experience, is my room, my bedroom, in here I close the door and it's like I closed the door of a vault to feel safe, protected and in where I can manage in a certain manner and comfortably my anxiety levels. We defend and take care of this sacred place with claw and teeth, we very rarely y let people enter freely because it disturb us and makes us feel that our privacy and only place in which our anxiety is relatively in check, has been violated.

It would be ideal to have many places like this one in our lives with OCD, because it would open a palette of physical places in which our anxiety and irrationality levels diminish considerably. For this reason I have taken the task, and I invite you to do the same, of identifying other places that can be "sacred" for us. For example, lately, when I enter my vehicle, my anxiety and obsessive levels diminish, reason why I'm trying to address this practice with the objective of having more than just one place in which I can feel comfortable.

For a strangers view, without experience and that has not lived what we live everyday with anxiety, this subject can seem banal and without importance; it could even be said that it contributes to the isolation of the OCD from the surroundings. What happens is that there is no more expert opinion than ours, because having a space in which we feel calm and tranquility, will let us recharge our mental strength for when we have to get out again to have the world and our anxiety, that we can scan the different thoughts and their irrational roots, what I mean is to do the ABC of deconstruction of diverse interactions and situations that happen to us daily. We with OCD have and need a huge doses of solitude (not abandonment), in which we can take a breather and make a change of mind toward rationality and positivity.

I want to repeat that not everyone feels this with their sacred places, I have known and had the placer of working with others with OCD that integrate third parties into this environments and use them as help in the process of pause and inclination towards our recognition of rationality.

In the next exercise I would like you to identify three potential "sacred" places and identify characteristic of them and why it would make easier to think rationally and diminish the anxiety levels. I want you to do this so you can realize that we can take these characteristics of these "sacred" places and transport them to other environments with the objective of augmenting our palette of possible physical places in which we can feel more comfortable.

Place 1:
CARACTERISTICS:

_____
_____
_____
_____

Place 2:
CARACTERISTICS:

_____
_____
_____
_____

Place 3:
CARACTERISTICS:

_____
_____
_____
_____
_____

26. OBSSESIVE THOUGHTS OR IDEAS RELATED WITH PHYSICAL DAMAGE

As we know the thought specter and palette of the OCD it's really wide and goes from an obsession to turn on and off the lights, to the symmetrical order of object, till random ideas or thoughts with obsessive and violent content. In my particular case this last type of thoughts haven't happened to me in my experience with different obsessions, but I do know witnesses of people that have this kind of thoughts so strongly and overwhelming that they prefer to stay at home fearing that they would happen. These thoughts can be: thinking something fatal is going to happen if I cross the street, thinking in hurting a loved one (even if we know we are not going to do it), obsessive and irrational ideas and/or thoughts about lies and cheating in a relationship, fear to go to sleep and never wake up, etc. There are many and this kind of thoughts can be very specific, but they have a common characteristic: we are 99.9 % certain that they are not true and that we are not going to do them. And it's that rational, numeric and statistical part that I need you to support so this kind of thoughts diminish their potency progressively. As always the ABC is fundamental, but also the oral expression of these thoughts with your therapist, with a trustworthy person or even with the people that is guilty or the victim in these thoughts. In this manner I assure you that you will leave a great weight and guilt load behind, that generally is accompanied by this kind of **totally irrational** ideas, and that have no evidence that they are actually going to happen in the moment or have a possibility to happen in the future. What I want you to do if you have this characteristics is to communicate as a coping mechanism and to be vigilant with the irrationality that overwhelms and causes you anxiety for no reason. We can have certainty that within the load of irrationality that we live everyday with OCD, this kind could be the biggest and as such the one that we have to give up sooner as possible through communication, exposition and observation of its false characteristics.

27. CAN WE WITH OCD HAVE A "NORMAL" LIFE?

Yes and no would be the answer, given that there is not something more subjective in this world than "normality". A more accurate question would be: can we with OCD have a lifestyle that's functional and healthy? Here the answer would be *yes, sure,* but as we know it all depends on you, your goals and your personal objectives and flexibility that you have to modify certain thought and action patterns that inhibit you from reaching that functional lifestyle. We with OCD want the world to work at our beck and call, something completely irrational, given that there are certain conventional rules that we have to accept as long as we want to work inside this system called society. This doesn't mean that you have to let go of all your routines of thought and action, but you will have to do a process of rearrangement and adjust sometimes towards the demands of society. In this last part the flexibility has an extremely important part, being capable of reorganizing our necessities according to what the outer world demands from us, **without stop being ourselves and keeping our identity.**

In the next exercise I want you to write down some rules and conditions that society imposes over you, and that you believe are not compatible with your lifestyle. I want you to identify them and ask: Cant I really arrange my thoughts and actions towards this demands? Could it be possible to rearrange and find balance?

LIST OF RULES AND CONDITIONS:

_____

_____

_____

_____

_____

_____

_____

Mark with an X the ones that you really think you cannot arrange in your lifestyle, and with the others I want you to rearrange them according to your style of functioning and daily routine.

Now I will like to expose the theoretical point of view of Dr. María Cristina Cavallini of the San Raffaele Cientific Institute, in the Neuroscience and Medicine Department of Milan University, given that somehow I share it and it provides an etiological perspective of the OCD.

According to Cavallini (2016) the Obsessive Compulsive Disorder (OCD) it's a psychological disorder of unknown etiology. The challenge in finding the etiology probably depends that in the phenotypic point of view, the OCD is a complex disorder.

Starting from the first decade of the XXI century, new investigations seem promising but so far without any conclusive hypothesis.

Besides the idiopathic forms of OCD, the obsessive-compulsive symptoms can be cause by a head trauma, encephalitis or pathological occurrences associated with the moment of birth, which suggests that specific brain lesions can be related to this disorder.

In the OCD we can describe various brain alterations evaluated using neurological image techniques (TAC, RMN, PET, SPECT) that hasn't given consistent results.

Even if the presence of critical lesions in some brain sections could determine the apparition of symptoms similar to those of the OCD, until now the true deficit or biological deficit and lesions or brain injuries that determined the idiopathic forms of OCD are unknown.

The pharmacologic experience brings some clues about the etiology of OCD. The patients with OCD are normally specifically benefited by a pharmacologic treatment in the long run, with serotonin reabsorption inhibitors, which suggest a favored participation of the serotonergic system, without being conclusive.

In this sense, the therapeutic response that results with clomipramine, a non-selective serotonergic medicine, supports the existence of a more complex sequence of interactions in different synaptic receivers (cholinergic, dopaminergic, etc.).

Some patients with OCD do not respond to the treatment with ISRS and only present a partial improvement after the addition of dopamine blockers to the treatment.

The dopaminergic theory in the OCD is sustained by different levels: the first one, the experimental animal models of OCD that include behaviors of a compulsive manner induced by the chronic administration of quinpirol, counterpart to the dopamine; the second, the human induction and exacerbation of the obsessive and compulsive symptoms related to the abuse of stimulants (amphetamines and cocaine), that cause the release of dopamine.

It has been proposed that OCD and Tourette syndrome (TS) belong to the same clinical specter, also other disorders like eating disorders, autism, etc. this advances the hypothesis that this disorders probably share some etiologic bases.

Even if it's true that the biological alterations can try to explain the OCD, there are diverse aspects that complicate this task. Probably the future definition of clinical homogeneous subgroups of patients, will make easier the identification of biological markers and ways of predicting response treatments.

This brief explanation from Cavallini provides us with answers to many questions, but at the same time it opens new doubts. We are never going to be able to know with certainty the exact cause of this disorder, nor the different environmental and genetic specific factors that develop it, but with time we will obtain a more holistic and complete view of the OCD.

28. THE OCD AND THE FAMILY

In general in a family there are certain demands, situations and events in which we must accomplish or assist as members of said social microsystem so important for every human being. In general, our behavior in the family and the particularities of this demand, are attended in a slightly minor percentage than those that are imposed by external social factors like work or social reunions with friends or colleagues, etc. This happens because inside our family system we "trust" and we can say many times "no" to certain events and invitations, given that it's a system relatively known and in where there is a sentimental meaning that justifies our decision. Something that we cannot do if for example our boss is asking something that goes out of our system or obsessive and compulsive routines, given that in general n a work relation you are tied to the accomplishment of certain rules or function if not you are fired. In the case of the family, we can play with the secondary profit of having OCD and we take advantage of our family feelings to justify our absence and get away with ours, like this we can get on with our obsessive and compulsive system as selfishly s it was programmed.

29. ANXIETY WITHOUT CAUSE OR "FLOATING" ANXIETY

With this kind of anxiety and this terminology I refer to that angst sensation, heart racing, sweating and incapacity to relax without specific evidence or cause of what is generating this state. This phenomenon is considered floating anxiety, and is cause and suffered above all for us with OCD, when we let our thoughts free reign in an overwhelming manner, we don't identify ourselves with the present, and in general our brain cannot see a cause for this state given the amount of stimuli. My answer to our brain and the explanation that I find is that what is happening, is happening in a time period in which our thoughts are completely irrational, we are thinking in future and/ or past time, and in general we have momentarily lost the capacity to do the appropriate ABC for the situation.

I know that these anxiety floating states happen to you frequently, that is why I want you to work with me in being able to diminish the frequency and intensity of this annoying mental state.

What I want you to do when you identify a lapse of floating anxiety is that you immediately set a **stop**, breathe deeply for five minutes, and if it's in your possibilities go to your sacred place, or some other place in which external stimuli is minor. Once you have done this these thoughts will still try to break into you, but we have something in our favor and that is that we have changed the physical space in which this phenomenon happened, allowing us to immediately tae a pencil and paper and make a *screening* or mental filter process in which you will classify all your thoughts according to their characteristics and/ or purpose, even if we know that most of them are irrational. With this what we achieve is to diminish in a potential manner the "unorganized" synapses between neurons and we can make a cognitive change towards an activity with an specified end that without you realizing it will substantially diminish your levels of floating anxiety. And also very important, we will travel first class and immediately from the past or future in which we were cognitively, towards the now, the present.

30. PRIORIZING OUR THOUGHTS

As someone with OCD we now that the obsessions and a great amount of intrusive thoughts are always going to be there, in greater or lesser intensity or frequency, depending on the tools that you have acquired to know how to handle this condition. Nor with this book nor with my professional expertise I pretend to find a panacea and eliminate the obsessions and compulsions completely. When I talk about priorizing our thoughts I mean to say that we have to prioritize and attend to the most important thoughts that we have, the rational ones that we continuously have.

For example, if in a specific moment of the day I have ten obsessive thoughts at the same time that are creating a lot of anxiety and I'm jumping from one to the other nonstop, want I want you to do it's to do a quick scan or filter of those thoughts that have an actual importance, meaning, the more rational ones. Following this same example if I have ten thoughts at the same time I'm going to evaluate my rationality levels and how important is each one with the objective of attending and focusing in the more relevant ones, while we put the other ones at the end of the list. With this I want to accomplish saving mental and cognitive energy and to provide a greater amount of strength and focus to the rational ideas or thoughts, leaving till last the ones that don't have worth, are toxic and as such, **irrational.**

Up next I want you to write the intrusive and obsessive thoughts that you have in this moment and that you score them from 1 to 10, being ten the ones with the most importance and rationality. Then I ask you to rearrange them, leaving in the last position the ones with the least importance. What I pretend with this is for you to focus your attention and energy in the first three thoughts with the greatest score and leave till the end the least important. You will realize that with this exercise you will lower your anxiety levels and diminish the irrational obsessions. At the end of the day you will realize that there were many thoughts at the end of the list that you didn't listen, and as such you focused in the ones that needed primary attention.

THOUGHT   SCORE
_____
_____

REARRANGEMENT LIST:

_____
_____

31. THE IMPORTANCE OF CONTROLLING THE COMPULSIONS FROM THE BEGGINING

Till this moment we have mainly emphasized the different characteristic, techniques and particularities of the obsessive part of the OCD, meaning the thoughts and anxiety that they produce us, but now I want to focus a little in the compulsions, meaning the behavioral manifestation of our obsessions or thoughts. Some of the abilities that we must train in an exhaustive manner are the different techniques and exercises that prevent us from making a reality of the compulsions related with determined thoughts. It's this important because we can obtain the necessary ability of stopping the compulsions, we would fill ourselves of a highly important self-control to be able to move forward and live with the OCD.

This subject about obsession control I introduce it in this segment because its closely related with priorizing obsessions. What I mean is that the compulsions or acts in which become a response to the main thoughts or obsessions, focusing there our greatest strength and dedication. For example in my case, one of the obsessions that I prioritize the least is the compulsive washing of my hands, because for me there are another palette of obsessions that I consider more important, for example my fixation on my face, a part of me that I don't allow anyone to touch and that I see in the mirror compulsively many times a day, so I can have a temporal 'relief' from the idea that my face is not perfect, or has a pimple or stain, etc. I have realized that the unlimited execution of the primary compulsions it's extremely related to the high possibility of them repeating many times a day without stopping the anxiety building, given that the compulsion doesn't work as a temporal relief. This means that while we think in a compulsive manner, we are getting the least amount of relief at the end, and this will turn in a spiral of growing anxiety and repetition of intrusive thoughts. Continuing with my example, if I start my day checking my face in the mirror without control, my obsession and compulsions that day will be out of control and I will be checking my face in any mirror or my reflection at least a hundred times a day. With this I want to help you understand that if one exercises control over our obsessions, avoiding the compulsive act from the beginning, we will fill ourselves with more cognitive strength and self-control with the objective of not repeating without stop the manifestation of compulsion of said obsession. As such when I wake up I focus in my face just for what need, after a shower for example, I fill myself with strength and I can have better control of not exercising the compulsion and because of that my anxiety levels diminish and I can focus my energies in something more productive and rational. I invite you to do this little exercise with your obsessions, being the most important ones o the least, what I want is that little by little we become capable of having more control over our thoughts and actions. I repeat: from the beginning of your day control at once the desire to make the specific compulsion, I assure you it will bring you great results.

32. THE IMPORTANCE OF WATCHING OVER AND MONITORING YOUR THOUGHTS

We know that the great majority of thoughts that happen during the day and introduce themselves in our cognitive patter are the rational and anxiogenic ones. Like many health campaigns expose "the best medicine towards decease is prevention", and in our case this is accurate. The prevention and proper attention of the intrusive irrational thoughts will save you a great quantity of psychological energy, it will lower the anxiety levels and will allow you to focus and be productive in the ideas and/or situations that are rational and need proper attention. With this I want to stimulate you to stop all the irrational thoughts, doesn't matter how "important" it is, because as a plant it will sprout and then grow, becoming stronger from irrationality, negativity and sabotaging your healthy and rational thoughts.

The only way to accomplish this is recovering one of the techniques that I gave you at the beginning of this book, and that is the importance of being in the present, in the now and not making anxiety filled trips to the future or depressive ones to the past. I repeat: the most important thing in our life, in which everything happens, it's the present, the now. In your case it would be to be reading these lines in this book, in this moment you are living, the now is the most important thing you have. Once we accomplish the development of this muscle that allows us being at least at 70% of our time in the present, it will be much easier to identify the appropriate way of recognizing any kind of irrational thought that's trying to reach your cognitive system with the objective of sabotaging your emotional state, your productivity and in general rob you of your peace and tranquility that you crave so much, but that you reach so rarely given that we have let irrational elements happen no matter their size or "relative" importance.

I want that in the next exercise you do a recount of the different thoughts that you have had in the last 24 hours and that have grown and augmented in their degree and capacity to alter your mental peace. Once you have identified these thoughts I would like you to write alongside that some kind of strategy that you could have used to stop them or don't allow them to begging.

THOUGHTS   STRATEGIES

_____

_____

_____

_____

_____

_____

_____

_____

In the strategies section I want you to write down some techniques with which we have been working till now: the ABC, thought priorizing, horse and rider technique, sacred place, among others.

33. OCD AND SOCIAL RELATIONS

According to the International Institute of Obsessive and Addicti-ve Disorders (IPITIA, 2006) if we suffer from an obsessive compulsive disorder its probable that we have an ambiguous relationship with others, what this means is that in various moments we don't know with certainty if we care about different people around us or If on the contrary, we have negative feelings towards them. We couldn't now with certainty if we want or not the company of these people (family, friends, etc.) people that we usually think that we care about but we could also be feeling exactly opposite frequently. For the person with OCD a relationship with others can be incomplete and inconstant, generating discomfort, frustration and anxiety.

With the help of an adequate psychological treatment the person with OCD can redefine its personal relationships in an internal mental level and take new decisions according to these relations (people with OCD tend to suffer difficulties to take decisions). People with OCD need to cut with everything that doesn't satisfy them or generates suffering; talking is necessary to clarify things with certain persons of their family, work or social circle; it needs to be alone; be more active and take the reins of his own life. Redefining his relationships with his surroundings the OCD tends to improve and disappear (IPITIA, 2006).

After what was exposed by the IPITIA in the last paragraph there is a relation between having OCD and general social relationships alterations. In my particular opinion I disagree with "OCD will eventually disappear", after the suggestions made by the institute. We have to be rational and understand that our tendency and obsessive and compulsive manifestations will be with us all our lives, in a minor or major degree, depending on the strategies, techniques and tools that you have to "manage" this disorder, but not to make it disappear.

The social relationships are a subject of great importance for the health of the subject to be able to interact with other individuals, given that as we were talking before the human being has four dimensions: psychological, physiological, spiritual and social. It's true that many times we tend to isolate ourselves and leave behind the social relationships for an irrational fear, like someone altering your functioning routine and because of that high levels of anxiety and stress would be generated. But we must understand that if we want to succeed in life in a work, family and couple level, we need to make certain behaviors and thoughts flexible, some that are extremely rigid and that make even harder our social interactions, even leading to depressive states created by ourselves due to loneliness and isolation. I invite you to do practice exercises with the objective of improving your social relationships, set for yourself a weekly challenge, in which you accept invitations that require mandatory social interactions. I know that at the beginning that triggers a lot of anxiety, but once that this saying no and being alone barrier has been broken, we will start liking this kind of interactions, benefiting our mental health, diminishing in a parallel manner the amount of intrusive and obsessive thoughts that we have, producing greater levels of endorphins that will make us feel better after such a long time of loneliness, anxiety and self-absorption.

34. THE ABILITIES THAT US WITH OCD MUST DEVELOP

All the human beings without exception must have a high degree of emotional intelligence to be able to survive and compete in today's society, one that is much more globalized and competitive. There are three primordial factors to us with OCD that we must develop and use often to be able to live in a determined society and also to be able to feel better physiologically and mentally, reducing the stress and anxiety levels.

As we know in the OCD the anxiety is the order of the day and it's for free, you can find it without problem. The elements that I want us to start to strengthen and use frequently are above all the ones we use in our relationship with our environment: assertive communication, resilience and patience. I assure you that each time that we strengthen these skills our lives will change both individually and inside society.

Now I will make a brief description of each of these skills and why they are so relevant in OCD context.

• Assertive communication: according Mayo (2012) the assertive communication is the skill to express ideas both positive and negative and the feelings that each individual has in an open, direct and honest manner. In this way both our rights and the rights of others are respected. It allows us to be responsible for ourselves and our actions without making other people responsible. More so it allows us to make constructive criticism and fin solutions to solve any kind of conflict.

This part is very important in OCD context because it permit us one way or another to manifest our way of thinking and feeling without insulting or upsetting the other person. With an assertive communication we can be capable of explaining to people that surrounds us the characteristics and particularities of certain thought and behavior patterns that could be seen or interpreted in a negative or strange manner given that they don't know the reasons why we behave that way or we constantly do things out of "normal" standards. Because of that the assertive communication its key to not be seen as "weird" beings, apart from certain social environments and also allowing us to diminish our anxiety levels because we have explained others the how and why we work in a very peculiar way, leaving behind the "secret" of our behavior.

- Resilience: according to Mayo (2012) the resilience is the capacity to face adversity and be able to adapt to tragedies, traumas, threats or severe stress.

To be resilient does not mean not to feel uncomfortable, emotional pain or difficulty in the face of adversity. Such as the death of a loved one, a serious disease, loss of a job, serious financial issues, etc. These issues can have a great impact in people, producing insecurity, uncertainty and emotional pain. Even so in general these people can get over these situations and adapt properly with time. This is resilience.

In the specific case of OCD, we are constantly battling with intrusive ideas and thoughts that try to sabotage our mental peace. Many times we are the accomplices of this avalanche of thoughts that grows non-stop till it unleashes a panic attack or a constant level of discomfort and restlessness. It's because of this that I want you to learn from this experiences in which you have self-sabotage yourself and you start to use all the techniques that I have given you with the objective of you being able to quickly identify and act toward the irrational thoughts that come to you in great quantities. You will see how with practice the frequency of the panic attacks or intense days in which you experience anxiety and restlessness will lower.

- Patience: according to Flores (2014) patience is the virtue of been able to handle with resignation the adversities, obstacles, offenses and other things, without lamenting. The word patience is from latin origin, it comes from the verb pati that means suffer, as such patience is reflected when a person can handle in silence disgusting situations.

I like this definition of patience because it includes the "resignation" term, a term that reflects one of the most powerful states of peace and tranquility that we can experience in our lives. For many people this term is negative and is related with weakness or loss, and is not that. When one resigns one acquires the great strength of being able of stop fighting over something or someone that will bring us a later positive result. It's a state of wisdom in which you stop fighting irrationally for something less valuable than the peace you could have in those moments.

That's has great importance for us with OCD because we develop and give strength to our capacity of being patient and resign those situations that are not worth a determined effort. We are constantly in a struggle of massive and irrational thoughts that have little value. That's why I ask you that we start practicing the ability to be patient and move aside those thoughts that demand a psychological effort that doesn't reflect how valuable is for us to be mentally at peace and tranquil. This implies the diminishing to the lest degree possible of the amount of thoughts and ideas, trying to be mostly rational and with a certain objective to fight for.

35. BEING ORIGINAL ABOVE ALL

Its nor weird at all that many of us have experienced and continue to experience being seen as a "weird bug", or that everyone is aware of our obsessive and compulsive routines. After many years of experience with OCD patients, and my own experience, I can tell you that very few people is interested in the things that we do, they are not even looking at us and they may have never realized that you have obsessive and compulsive patterns. But then, why do I feel and think that people is staring at me? Simple: because you are conscious that what you are doing are repetitive behavior patterns generally compulsive, which you do to momentarily diminish the anxiety of your obsession. As such the one that is staring and labeling yourself as a "weird bug" is yourself, you already know that your behavior patterns are out of the ordinary, irrationals and generating great quantities of stress and anxiety.

I bring this up to help you diminish one more factor in your anxiety palette, that one of believing that you are being observed all the time and that people is looking at you funny, etc. Don't, eliminate from your thoughts all that kind of irrational obsession. You already know how it happens now I need you to practice the technique in which every time you feel this kind of thought coming and the anxiety starts building up, stop them quickly and give yourself the same irrational explanation of what's happening to you. Remind yourself, statistically you are not seen as a bad person, you are not more remarkable that any other guy in the population. Erase from yourself that "weird bug" label and think that you are the center of attention.

Having said this, I want you to act like yourself and to feel your obsessions and compulsions controlled with the help of all these techniques, without interrupting your original and honest way of being, your own kind of being. The obsessions and compulsions are a couple of factors with which you will have to live your entire life, and as such they form a big part of your personality, of course as long as you control the levels of obsession and compulsion and you are aware of them and how to make them companions and friends to your life, instead of trying to fight them irrationally in war that you know you are going to lose. Here is important to remember the concept of resignation and acceptance of the reality of your life. What we are not going to do is having obsessions and compulsions that are of no use at all, they are filled with irrationality and little relevance or importance in a daily bases. It's because of this last part that I like to refer to myself as an OC, and I have expressed so in this book. I am and you are OC and that makes us unique, different and very valuable.

Up next I would like to provide you with a fragment of a diary of a patient with OCD in which he shares his ten basic life lessons to those of us with that disorder.

Lesson 1: LOVE YOURSELF

OCD made me believe that I wasn't adequate, that I was like a toy that had a piece missing, someone imperfect that didn't deserve happiness, joy or being appreciated by others. This feeling is sadly common in all human beings in some point in their existence, when this blooms it's primordial to reconnect with the sense of worth. Remember that you are valuable, different, unique and is worth it to be oneself.

From the beginning there has never been in this planet anyone just like you and there never will be. You are a unique person, special, that has its own virtues and capacities. No one can do things exactly like you do them, as such there is not a competition or comparing. You are a magnificent being worthy of your 0own love and acceptance...

I remember that when I first read these words from Louis Hay I cried like a child...

Lesson 2: DON'T JUDGE OTHERS

We usually judge others too son (and ten to be mistaken most of the times). Everyone is enduring an inner struggle in which, in most cases, we have no idea whatsoever.

Try to see beyond appearances. Not only because of others wellbeing but for your own.

We can never judge other peoples life, because we only know about our own pain and resignation. One thing is to think that one is in the right path other is to assume that path is the only one.

Paulo Celho

Lesson 3: UPDATE YOURSELF (FREE YOURSELF FROM THE PAST)

I compare our minds with software that has to be constantly updated (sometimes daily) so it works correctly. What does it means to update our min? It means to let go of the weight of the past (guilt, remorse, the "it could have been better if...") to be truly free. Like that the "software" can work without getting stuck, flowing completely updated with the present time connected to "what you are today" (and that would be the latest system available) and not conditioned to what you were yesterday.

No one but ourselves can free our minds from slavery.

Bob Marley

Lesson 4: GET BUSY (STOP WORRYING ABOUT THE FUTURE)

When you have OCD the constant threat that something horrible is going to happen if you don't repeat this or that is always there.

But that fear it's not our sole property. We are genetically designed to act in favor of our survival. The problem is that most times the threats under which we act exist only in our heads.

Try hard to distinguish between the real threats and the "imaginary" ones. We often act pushed by a threat that doesn't actually exist. And worst of all, we put conditions to our existence parting from a fear that we ourselves have created.

You choose who you are daily. Choose wisely. Choose to anchor yourself in the here and now.

Live anchored to the only moment over which you have real power: the present time.

Yesterday is history. Tomorrow is a mystery. But today is a gift...that's why is called present.

Oogway (Kung Fu Panda)

Lesson 5: LIFE IS UNCERTAIN (ACCEPT IT)

Life is an adventure. And as all adventures it's uncertain. Anything can happen. It's impossible to have it all under control. Give up trying to control everything around you. Stop trying to take control over the safety of all that surround you, over your environment, over the world...its madness.

Instead of that, accept life's invitation to be a part of this great adventure. That doesn't mean that you will live without responsibilities or crossing the street without checking both sides. Accept your responsibilities and honor them (of course) but free yourself from the rest of things that are not your responsibility and trust the best outcome to happen.

I thought it was and adventure and in reality it was life.

Joseph Conrad

Lesson 6: IF YOU LIVE, YOU ARE GOING TO MAKE MISTAKES (ACCEPT IT)

As someone with OCD there is an infinite number of times in which –making a "mistake"- I have been stuck in an endless compulsion about the "right" choice till exhaustion. The disorder pushed me to search for perfection in every action of daily life. The towel had to be "perfect", I had to pick it up in the "perfect" manner, dry myself up in the "perfect" way... and if I didn't do each and every last of these things in the "perfect" way I had to start again. It was a nightmare in real life.

Our society pushes us to search for absurd perfection. And I say absurd because this perfection it doesn't have anything to do with professional or personal excellence. Let's remember that often the great findings of humanity have happened from imperfections or things that looked like mistakes and almost all the time that we learn a lesson in a personal level is because we did a mistake. Don't avoid the mistake. Instead of that be wrong in a better way.

Life is so interesting, if you do mistakes.

Georges Carpentier

Lesson 7: THE WORLD IS IMPERFECT (ACCEPT IT TOO)

The world is chaotic, asymmetric and disorganized. And it's perfect like that. Accept it. Don't make yourself the attendant of the cosmetic section of your blocks market or be obsessed for having an extremely organized house. Embrace your own imperfection and find the magical beauty behind it. Does this mean not to try to improve? Not at all. It means that a little bit of imperfection is necessary in everything healthy.

Allow some imperfection to exist. It's like having trash can at home. It's ok to have a trash can in a corner of your house. If you don't want to have a trash can, all your house will be a trash can...

Sri Sri Ravi Shankar

Lesson 8: FACE YOUR FEARS

When you have OCD fear literally reins your life. To break this fear vicious cycle you have to face it.

In this society we are often taught to live with fear. Living with fear and like that buying everything they are trying to sell us. Living with fear and not saying what we think so we are not fired from our jobs. Living with fear is terrible.

Choose each day to live without fear.

Life is and adventure as I said before. Get out of your "comfort zone" and trust into your "learning zone". See beyond that. That zone that for many is called "panic area" it's actually a "magic zone" in where anything can happen.

Watch in this video what happens when this little girl faces her fears, she enters her learning area and goes beyond. It's magical.

Life is wonderful if you are not afraid of it.

Charles Chaplin.

Lesson 9: BE OPTIMISTIC

If you find yourself hypothesizing over possible future lines, consciously choose to think in the positive one. If you think you are not naturally optimistic be conscious of the fact that you can choose your own thoughts and change that tendency in yourself. Very often I have heard "I'm a natural pessimist". I don't think such a thing exists. I think we choose to be who we are at each moment. Choose wisely positive thoughts over the negative ones. They will light your paths towards success.

Optimism is the faith that leads to success. Nothing can be done without faith and hope.

Hellen Keller

Leseson 10: BELIEVE (IN YOURSELF AND YOUR INNER MIGHT)

You are way stronger that you can imagine. Like the famous saying says "you never know how strong you are until being strong is your only option".

You have to have faith. If you don't believe in god, believe in the supreme energy, in the source, in life, in the angels, in the stars, in the spirit guide, in fairies or in whatever you feel as true in your heart. But believe. Faith is necessary. We need to believe to be able to live.

To believe is to live and to live is to believe.

Roque Barcia

36. HOW DO I GET OUT OF THE VICIOUS CYCLE OF OBSESSIVE THOUGHTS WHEN THINGS DON'T HAPPEN AS EXPECTED?

We with OCD have a scheduled life with certain action patterns that require a systematical accomplishment of diverse tasks with the objective of having gratification (usually momentarily) for having accomplished our rigid schedule. Meaning, our daily plan is to accomplish the previously established tasks and our satisfaction is going to be linked to the accomplishment percentage of those tasks. In our own experience we know that we never or almost ever are going to accomplish the 100% of the tasks that we have set, or at least not in the way that we had thought, this happens because the life that surrounds us is unpredictable and doesn't have the obligation to adapt to our selfish requirements or demands.

With this I want you to understand that every day you are going to suffer one way or another, in greater or lesser quantity, "disappointments" and spikes in your anxiety levels and in the amount of intrusive thoughts, because of that I need you to accept and resign to this reality called life. I know that when things don't come out as we desire our anxiety spikes and our irrational thoughts levels climb to the clouds, searching for possible useless solutions with the objective of accomplishing your rigid schedule of task planning of daily activities. I'm sorry, life doesn't work like that, I want that when things don't come out as you planned you adopt resignation and acceptance mode and receive with open arms and mind the new situation that's presenting itself, one that if you permit it can be even more beneficial that the one you have previously programmed. I'm not asking you to stop programming your day or your life I'm only asking you not to get stuck and arising your anxiety levels when things don't happen as they should, because it's not only unhealthy for you, but also it will paralyze you and you won't be able to accomplish with your other objectives. You can see how this is a two edged sword that will make you responsible for not being able to accomplish your schedule given that it will stuck you, because you didn't accept the situation nor you resigned yourself and you couldn't turn the page and move on. From now onwards I want that things don't happen as you expect them, accept it, resign to it, learn from it and move on to your next objective in the plan.

Up next I would like you to do a list of at least three situations that happen to you in the last two weeks that after you analyzed them you realize you got stuck and paralyzed because you weren't able to accept and resign about the reality of life. I also want you to write down the irrational thoughts associated with these circumstances.

PARALIZING SITUATION IRRATIONAL THOUGHTS

37. DON'T TAKE LIFE SO SERIOUSLY, PLAY AND LAUGH

We with OCD believe that every decision that we take or everything that doesn't come happen as planned is a catastrophe, and as such it would bring important consequences, our anxiety levels arise and we become even more obsessive and compulsive with the objective of correcting the consequences of any "mistake" or situation that gets out of our perfectly established limits about what's right. Well no my friend, not every situation in life and I would dare say even than less than the 10% of them are decisions with serious and transcendental consequences. As such that 90%

left we have to enjoy it and live it in the most fun, spontaneous and funny way possible, something that we with OCD don't do, and we believe that 100% of life and our decisions have a transcendental value and as such one has to be alert 24 hour a day, including sleep. In one moment in this world we have expiration date and it in your hands the power to choose in what way and in what emotional state you are going to face life. Do you want to live in a state of constant tension and permanent alert? Well, go forward, but I assure you are not going to be happy, or would you rather take life as it comes and accept it as it is only visualizing that 10% like the serious part with transcendence and vital importance? I assure you that if you choose the second option, the one I have chosen to live since years past, it will make things easier and will diminish your anxiety levels exponentially. Now I know that not everything I do or decide has to be measured and said with precision, I know that life is filled with imperfections that make it as it is. I need you to visualize your life and that of those that surround you and care about and see it as a game in which only a small percentage of the time you have to put the pants on and be serious. We as OC wake up with our hair as a mess and claws ready to attack, instead of allowing ourselves to be grateful we have one more day as an opportunity to participate in this game filled with things, people and beautiful situations that filled us as human beings.

38. THE "VICTIM" PAPER AND THE SECONDARY PROFIT

As I have described before in several of this book passages we the OC have a great intellectual capacity and as such a great ability to manipulate. When we use our symptoms and characteristics as OCD in our lives as an excuse to get away or release from commitments that we don't want to do this is called secondary profit. And it doesn't only happen in the case of us with OCD, in general everyone one way or another in a greater or lesser degree use this strategy to "get away with ours". Yes I have to admit that in our case we make a greater use of this secondary profit, because we try to evade and escape this commitments that can alter one way or another our previously established schedule of obsessive and compulsive routines. I bring this system up because I have realized that the more we use the secondary profit mechanism, and we adopt the "victim" role in any way, we are perpetuating and intensifying our obsessive and compulsive symptoms generating even more anxiety. I need you to help me to help you, and as such I want you to make a list of situations in which you use or have used the secondary profit system or have adopted the role of the victim, also detecting what positive elements would it bring you to take that challenge or responsibility; I also want you to be aware so when a situations presents itself in which you can perpetuate this mechanism, you provide a different answer, accepting the challenge or invitation, exposing yourself to the anxiety of getting out of your comfort zone. I only as you to do this progressively and start taking more risks little by little with the objective of diminishing your anxiety levels created by irrational thoughts or routines and also so you can train for the moment in which you have to take even greater responsibilities like relationships, marriage, kids, work, school, projects, etc. situations that have characteristics and responsibilities that will not always adapt to your rigid cognitive process.

39. MAKE ANXIETY YOUR GREATEST ALLY

It's true that the most recent editions of the DSM 5 or Mental Disorders Diagnostic Manual the OCD takes a whole category for itself, while in previous editions it belonged to anxiety disorders, a purview that I share. There is no doubt that when we talk about OCD or want to explain others what happens to us THE ANXIETY as a mental or emotional state takes a lead role. Having OCD is having ANXIETY , as simple as that or as complex as you want to see it. The anxiety present in this disorder is caused by yourself, you have created it and you have to face it like you want to face it, depending in the cognitive tools that you have and your motivation to change or stay in your "comfort" zone in which you are accustomed. Let's be honest, none of us likes to live with anxiety, it's uncomfortable, annoying, paralyzing and robs us a great capacity to act or be spontaneous. It's because of that we the OC are known or seen by other people as boring, predictable, square, repetitive, cowards, etc. And yes they are right, because we have an immense fear to face the anxiety that lives in us 24 hours a day.

CONCLUSION

In this book I have presented to you several strategies and techniques that will make easier the approach and recognition of your anxiety and as such be able to beat it in numerous occasions. At the end my intention will always be for you not to run away from anxiety, instead identify it, search for its reason of being, get close to it and above all destroy it or make it your best friend with the different strategies that I have presented you in this book.

There are no magical cures, shortcuts or easy exits to beat the anxiety or to live without OCD, we have to accept and resign to the fact that is something with which we will live all our lives, and that it can be your greatest ally if we know how to recognize it and take benefits from this disorder, or it can be our worst enemy if we let it to take over our lives and act passively towards it.

I will like to end this first contact with you, OCD colleagues, inviting you to a second contact or continuation of this book or life manual for people that live in one way or another with this disorder.

I want you to take this with you and try to apply it every day:

1. I'm capable of modifying my irrational thoughts and situations for those that are more rational and healthy for me.
2. I'm the creator of my own anxiety and as such I can keep it alive or destroy it or make it my greatest companion.
3. My characteristics as someone with OCD can benefit me if I know how to recognize them, identify them and channel them for my own good.
4. Life is unpredictable, as such I will try to be at least 70% of the time in the present moment, in the now.

BIBLIOGRAPHY

1. American Psychiatric Association. (2013). Diagnostic and sta-tistical manual of mental disorders (5th ed.). Washington, DC: Author.
2. Cavallini, M.(2012). Bases biológicas del Trastorno Obsesivo Compulsivo. Instituto de Altos Estudios Universitarios. Facultad de Medicina de Milán.
3. Hayon, S. (2010). Características de las relaciones de pareja en pacientes Obsesivos y Compulsivos. Un estudio de caso. Tesis de Graduación. U. Latina. Costa Rica.
4. Mayo. G. (2012). La inteligencia Emocional del Ser Humano. Editorial Poas. Quito, Ecuador.
5. Fores, J. (2012). Factores que benefician la paz mental. Editorial Poas. Quito, Ecuador.